My Magic Show

Dawn McMillan
Photography by Siân Bradfield

Contents

Magic is Fun

Hi, I'm Amber and I think magic is fun! I have loved magic ever since I learnt about Harry Houdini. He is my favourite magician.

Houdini became a magician in 1891. He did card tricks and other magic tricks, such as making an elephant disappear! Houdini was also an amazing escape artist.

In one of Houdini's most famous escapes, he was handcuffed and his legs were tied in chains. Then, he was placed in a wooden crate.

The crate was locked and lowered into the water. Everybody held their breath ... but Houdini managed to break free. Wow!

My Magic Tricks

My magic tricks are different to Houdini's. They're not as dangerous, but I think they're a lot more fun!

This afternoon, my grandparents are coming to visit. I'm going to do some of my new magic tricks for them. I can't wait!

I have my magician's outfit on – a magician's hat, a cape and a magic wand.

My magician's table is ready, too.
All of my **props** are on it.

I have to practise my magic tricks before my grandparents arrive. If you promise not to tell anyone, I'll show you how they work...

The Magnetic Pencil

What I need:

- a pencil

What I do:

1. I put the pencil on the table.
2. I say, "I can make this pencil stick to my hand."
3. Next, I squeeze my right wrist with my left hand. I rest my right hand on the pencil and say "Magic magneto!"
4. I raise my right hand and the pencil sticks to it!

How Does It Work?

When I rest my right hand on the pencil, I secretly slip my index finger from my left hand under the pencil.

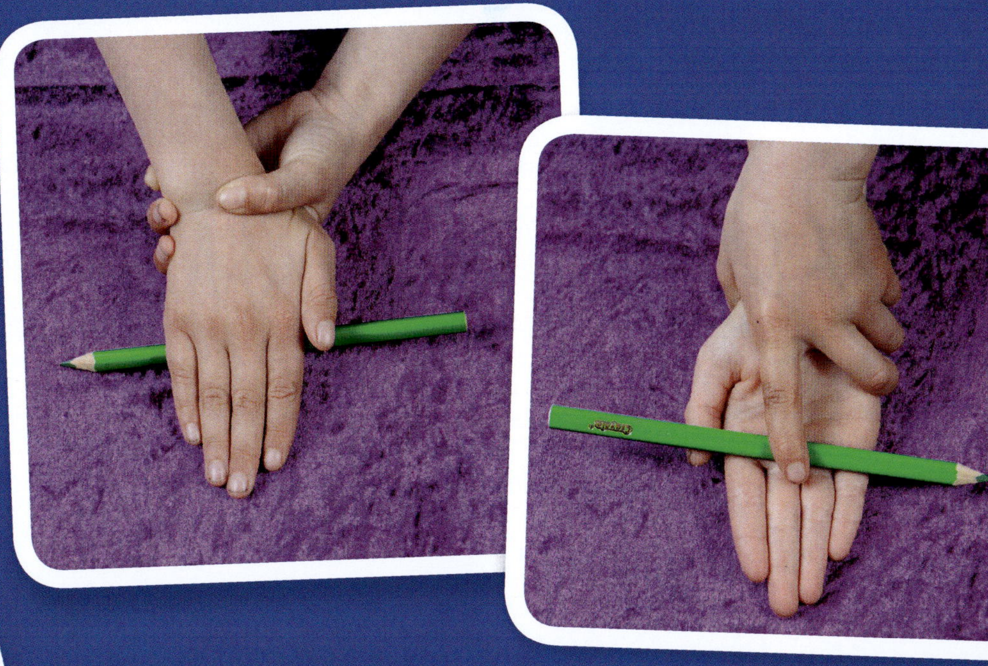

I make sure the audience doesn't see this, so it looks like the pencil is sticking to my hand.

Ta da!

I Know Your Number

What I need:

- a sheet of blank paper
- 1 pencil or pen
- 3 **volunteers**

What I do:

1. I fold the paper long-ways into three parts.
2. I tear the paper along the folds.
3. I give the middle piece of paper to a volunteer. They write a number on it. Then, they fold it up.
4. I give the other two pieces of paper to the other volunteers. They do the same.

5. I put the three folded pieces of paper into my hat.
6. I ask the first volunteer to **concentrate** on their number.
7. I wave my wand over my hat.
8. I pull out one piece of paper from my hat. It's their number – shazam!

How Does It Work?

Before I give the middle piece of paper to the first volunteer, I tear two rips in it. Then, when I reach into my hat, I feel for the paper with the rips and pull it out.

Ta da!

The Magic Rope

What I need:

- a piece of rope

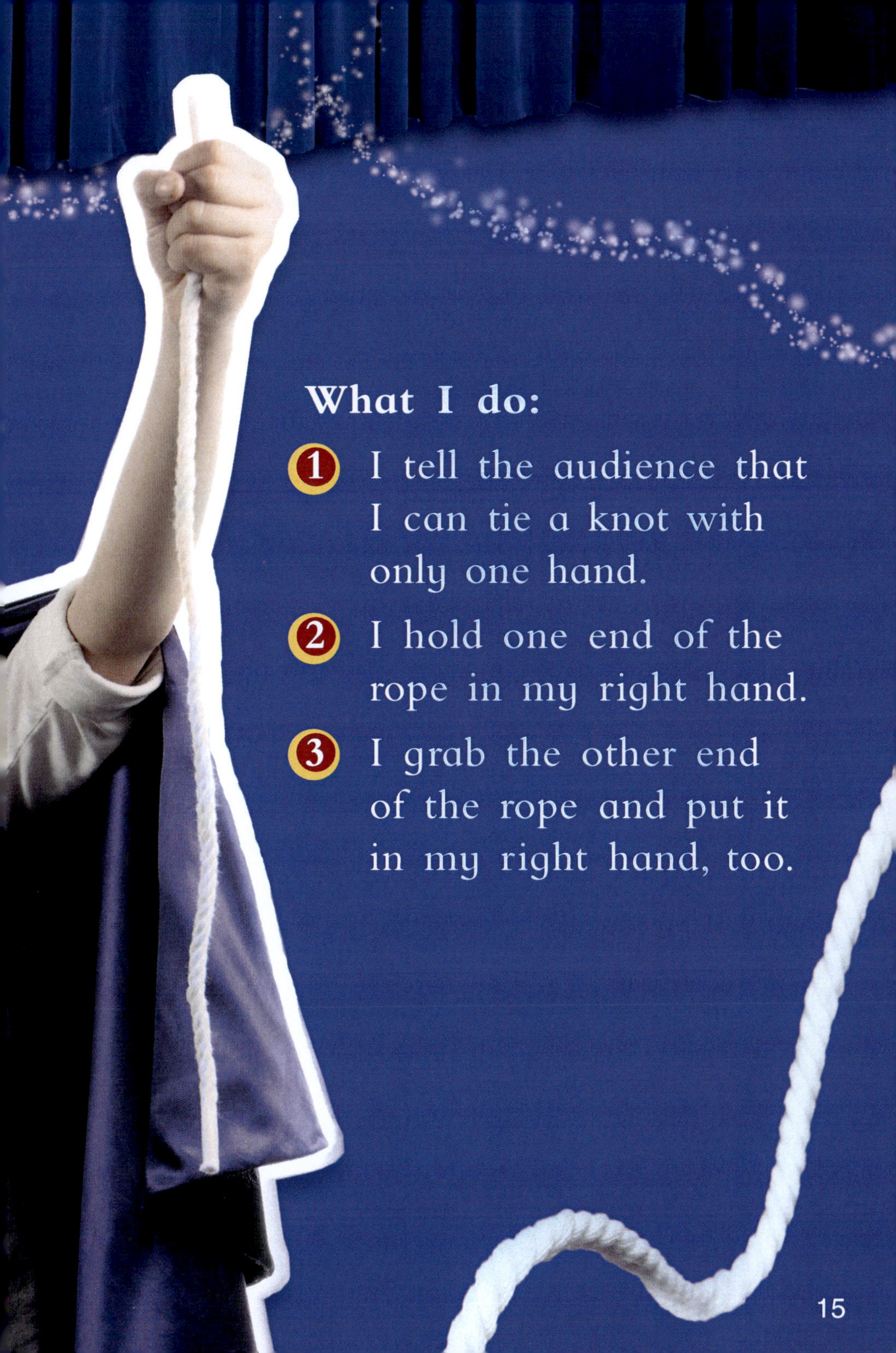

What I do:

1. I tell the audience that I can tie a knot with only one hand.
2. I hold one end of the rope in my right hand.
3. I grab the other end of the rope and put it in my right hand, too.

4 I shake the rope. Then, I blow on it.

5 I drop one end of the rope. There's a knot in it – isn't that clever!

How Does It Work?

Before I start, I tie a knot in one end of the rope. The knot is hidden in my right hand. Then, I make sure I drop the knotted end of the rope.

This magic trick may sound easy but it's not. It needs a lot of practice!

The Clipped Queen

What I need:

- five cards (one of the cards must be a queen)
- glue
- a paperclip
- a volunteer

What I do:

1. I place the five cards together in a row. The queen is in the middle. Then, I glue the cards together.
2. I show the cards to the volunteer and tell them to remember where the queen is.

3. I turn the cards around. I ask the volunteer to put the paperclip on the queen.

4. I say the magic word "Abracadabra" and turn the cards around. The paperclip is not on the queen in the middle. It is on the card at the end!

How Does It Work?

This magic trick is very simple. The way the cards overlap looks different from the front view to the back view. The front view shows the queen covered by the seven and the five. When you turn the cards over, the queen is covered by the ten and the three.

Change the Arrow

What I need:

- a glass
- some paper that has been folded in half with an arrow drawn on it (make sure the paper is a bit shorter than the glass)
- a jug of water

What I do:

1. I put my card on the table. The audience can see the arrow.
2. I put the glass in front of the card.

3. I tell the audience that I can make the arrow flip without touching the card.

4. I pour the water into the glass. The arrow flips over – bam!

How Does It Work?

Adding water to the glass turns it into a **lens**. The lens makes the arrow look like it has flipped and changed direction!

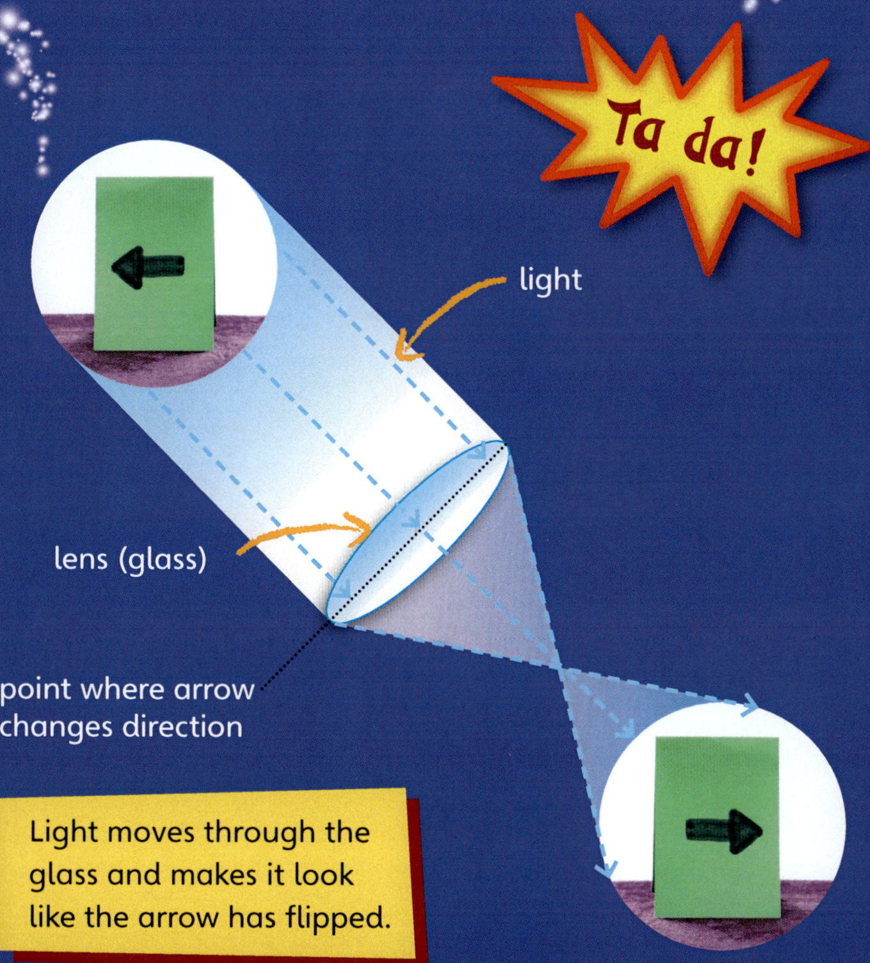

Light moves through the glass and makes it look like the arrow has flipped.

The Vanishing Bead

What I need:

- 1 paper cup
- 2 beads (the same colour)

What I do:

1. I hold the paper cup.
2. I put a bead into the cup.
3. I flip the cup upside down. The bead has gone!
4. I put my other hand in my pocket and ... I pull out the bead – hey presto!

How Does It Work?

Before I start, I cut a hole in the bottom of the cup. I also put one of the beads in my pocket. When I flip the cup upside down, the first bead falls through the hole into my hand. Then, I grab the second bead from my pocket and show the audience.

Dad helped me cut the hole in my cup. Make sure you get an adult to help you, too.

Show Time!

My grandparents are here! Everything is ready for my magic show. I'm so excited but a little bit nervous, too.

I take a deep breath...
let the show begin!

Glossary

concentrate	to pay close attention
lens	a clear piece of glass or plastic that changes the light passing through it, causing objects to look different
props	items used in a show or a play
volunteers	people who help others without getting paid